KT-504-820

great new ways with granny squares

Rosa P.

Search Press

granny squares

Crocheting is the new yoga. It's relaxing, easy to learn, and you can do it anywhere. All you need is a ball of wool and a crochet hook.

The projects are fresh and modern with a trendy, retro feel. They can be made anywhere. I like to crochet on the train, in waiting rooms, on park benches, sitting on my sofa and sometimes even in the pub. It's a great way to chill out.

Choose chain stitch instead of the lotus pose. Or perhaps chain stitch in the lotus pose – you decide!

Rosa P.

rosa-r.blogspot.de

Acknowledgements

My thanks to Annelore, Janina, Claudia and Isabell the tireless 'needlers' without whom this book would not have been possible.
Also, thanks to my editors and to my wonderful models, Lisa and Monja.

Levels of difficulty

* = quick and easy
** = easy
*** = average
**** = requires some practice
***** = more challenging/requires more time

great new ways with granny squares

First published in Great Britain in 2015 by Search Press
Wellwood, North Farm Road, Tunbridge Wells, Kent, TN2 3DR

Original edition © 2013 Christophorus Verlag GmbH & Co. KG, Freiburg
World rights reserved by Christophorus Verlag GmbH & Co. KG, Freiburg
Original German title: *Granny Squares Postmodern*

Designs: Rosa P. (alias Ulrike Pacholleck)
Contributors: Rosa P. (pages 22, 30, 34, 46, 50, 60), Claudia Busshardt (pages 38, 54),
Janina Frank (pages 14, 32, 48), Isabell Heiny (pages 26, 42),
Annelore Schellberg (pages 16, 18, 20, 36, 44, 56, 58)
Photographs: Florian Bilger
Styling: Monika Arlow
Crochet patterns and diagrams: Carsten Bachmann
Tutorial drawings: Brigitte Fischer

All rights reserved. No part of this book, text, photographs or illustrations may be reproduced or transmitted in any form or by any means by print, photoprint, microfilm, microfiche, photocopier, internet or in any way known or as yet unknown, or stored in a retrieval system, without written permission obtained beforehand from Search Press.

ISBN: 978-1-78221-149-5

Suppliers

If you have difficulty in obtaining any of the materials and equipment mentioned in this book, then please visit the Search Press website for details of suppliers: www.searchpress.com

Printed in China

Contents

Good to know

The crochet hook

You can buy crochet hooks made of plastic, aluminium, bamboo, metal and wood. Whatever you choose, the hook should be absolutely smooth to prevent the yarn from catching. A straight handle with no fancy bits sits well in the hand. The thickness or size of the hook is given in millimetres ranging from 0.6 to 15mm in Europe, with the corresponding sizes in the USA being 14 to Q. The thicker your yarn or wool, the thicker the hook needs to be.

The yarn

We used the widest range of yarns for the designs in this book: wool, alpaca, cotton, silk, linen, cashmere, viscose – from very thin to very thick. The choice of yarn makes every item unique and decides the function; cotton is ideal for hard-working items such as bags, whereas alpaca is nicer for a snuggly poncho. Silk is used for exclusive items such as a glossy plaid, and fine merino wool is the easy-to-use, all-purpose choice for any occasion. Cashmere can be a part of a glamorous stole or wrap, but can also be used for the star on the sofa throw.

The colours

Colours are what will make your work unmistakable.
Soft and pastel colours for spring.
Strong and bright colours for summer.
Vivid ambers and browns for autumn.
Cool and understated colours for winter.
Or to suit your own taste and temperament. The choice is yours!

The symbols

Far from being a kind of secret code, once learnt they make crocheting easy and uncomplicated. Every crochet pattern includes an explanation of the symbols in which each one represents a particular stitch. Every symbol represents one stitch, every line or round of symbols a line or round of stitches.

- · = 1 chain
- ⌒ = 1 slip stitch
- I = 1 single crochet (UK double)
- T = 1 half double crochet (UK half treble)
- † = 1 double crochet (UK treble)

Reading a crochet pattern

In rounds

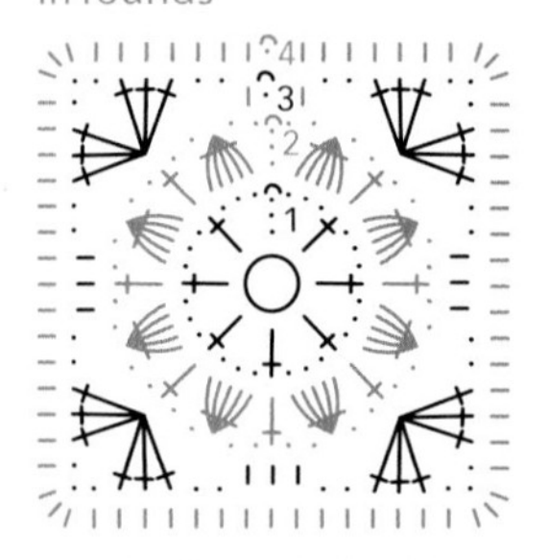

Items that are worked in rounds are always worked from the inside to the outside, anti-clockwise – and accordingly, the rounds of symbols are read from left to right. Start each round with the corresponding number of chains to stand for the first stitch, and slip stitch to the top replacement stitch (or the first stitch of the previous round). Work 1 chain to replace single (UK double) crochet, 2 chain to replace a half double crochet (UK half treble), and 3 chain for double crochet (UK treble) and relief double crochet (relief trebles).

In rows

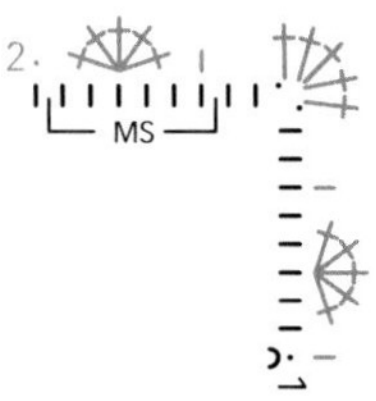

Borders crocheted in rows are worked from bottom to top. The first stitch of every row is replaced by chain: work 1 chain for a single (UK double) crochet, 2 chain for a half double crochet (UK half treble), and 3 chain for double crochet (UK treble) and relief double crochet (UK treble).

Corners

When working corners, generally we work several stitches into the corner or additional chain.

Changing the colours

Work a slip stitch to add a new colour. These joining slip stitches are always shown in the patterns in this book.

Joined symbols

If a number of symbols are joined at the bottom in a crochet pattern, it means that the corresponding stitches are worked into the same stitch. If the stitches are joined at the top, it means that the corresponding stitches are decreased together.

Basic crochet course

Casting-on in chain stitch

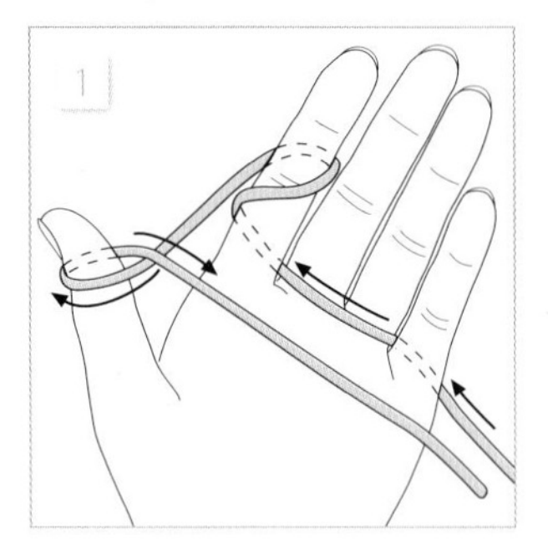

Wind the yarn around your left hand as shown in the illustration.

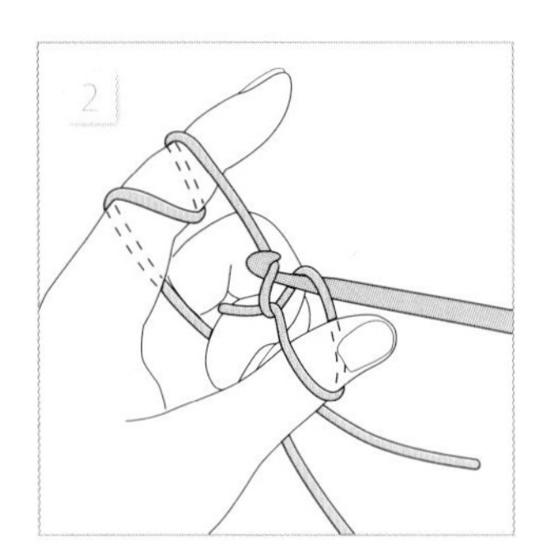

Push the hook into the thumb loop from below. Take up the yarn and draw through. Remove your thumb from the loop. You have completed the casting-on knot and one loop.

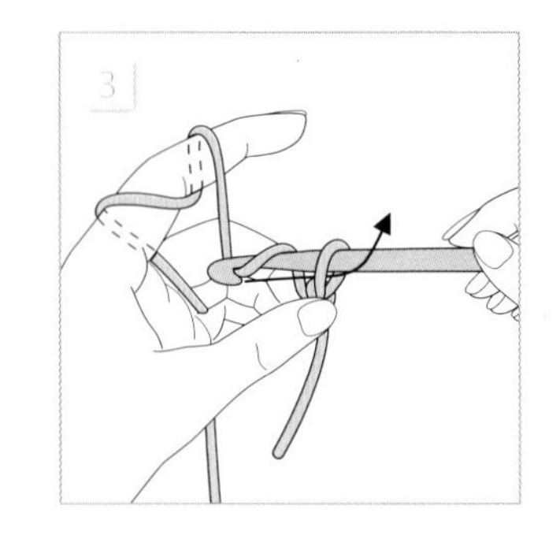

Hold the casting-on knot between your thumb and middle finger. Take up the thread around your index finger with the hook and draw through the loop.

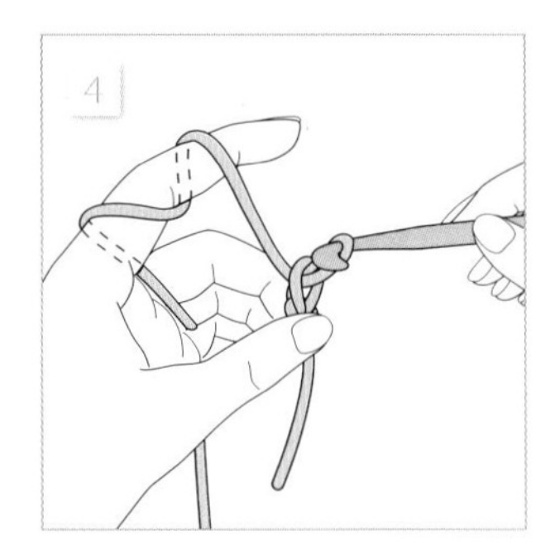

You have completed the first chain. Repeat until you have worked the required number of chain stitches.

Chain stitch ring

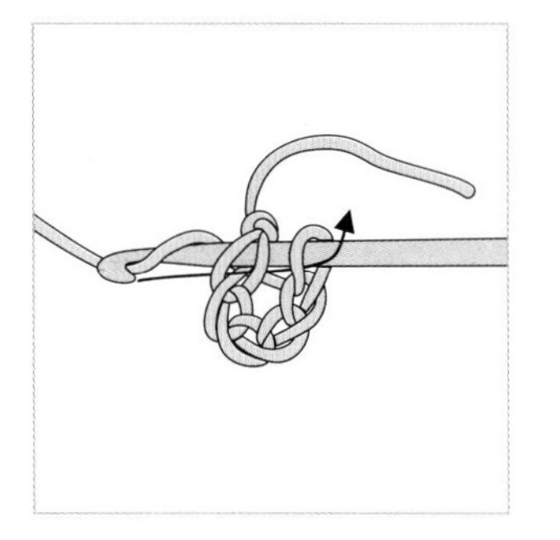

Crochet the required number of chain stitches. Work 1 slip stitch into the first chain to close the ring.

Magic ring

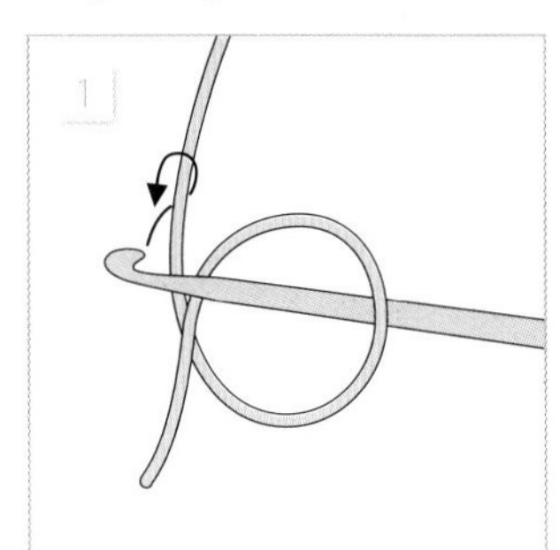

Fold the yarn in a loop, insert hook, …

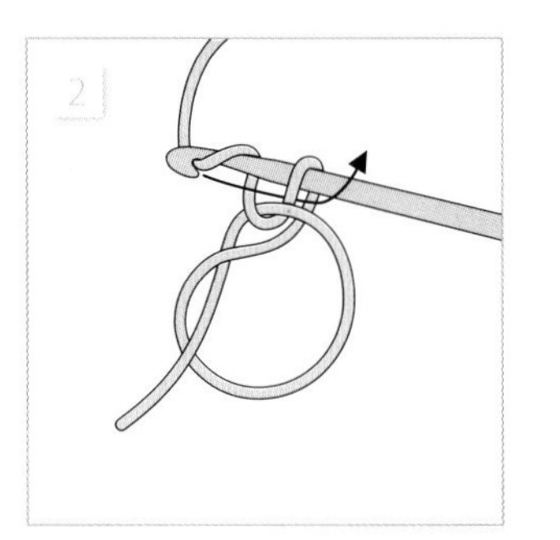

… yarn over hook and draw through. Don't pull it tight! Place the working yarn around the left index finger. Hold the crossover point of the ring, draw yarn through the loop on the hook.

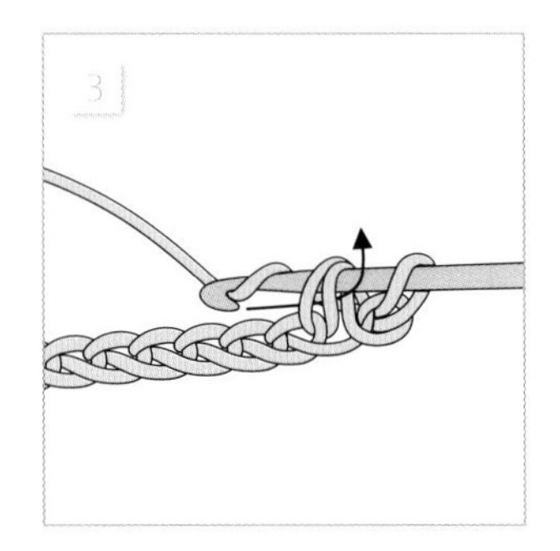

Continue like this to work the required number of stitches (in this case, for example, we are using treble crochet/ UK double treble) into the ring. Pull the yarn loop tight. Fold the yarn twice to make a double loop when required.

Single crochet (UK double)

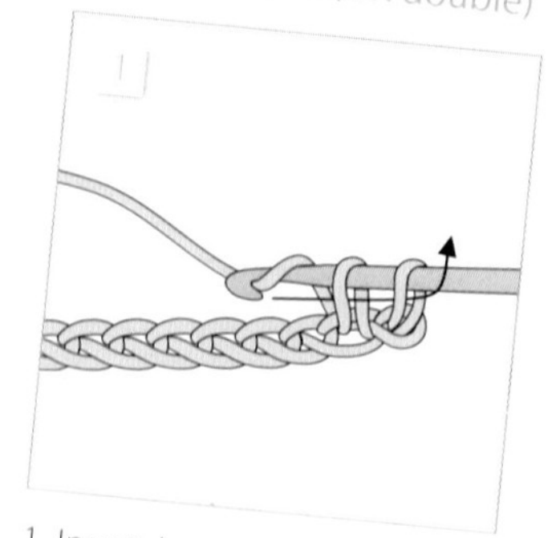

1 Insert hook in the intended stitch and bring yarn over the hook from back to front.

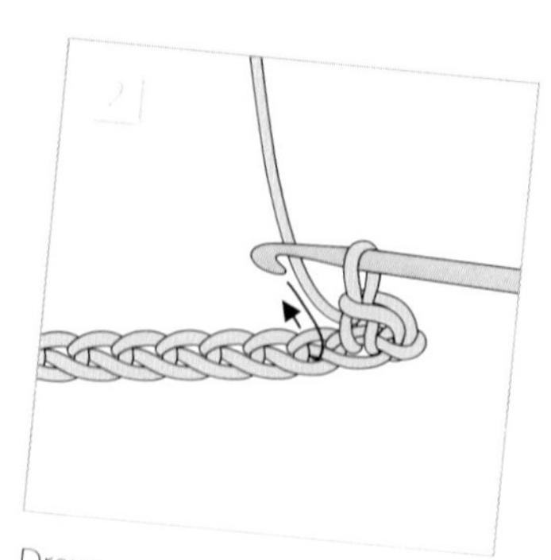

Draw yarn through. Yarn over hook and draw through both loops.

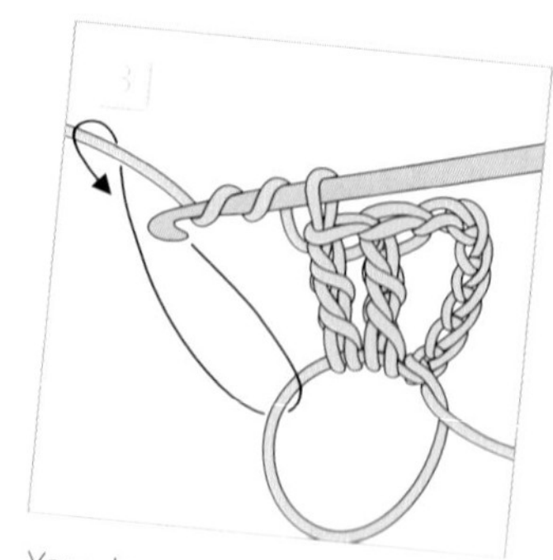

You have worked your first single (UK double) crochet. Repeat steps 1 and 2 until you have completed the row.

Work into back loop of stitch

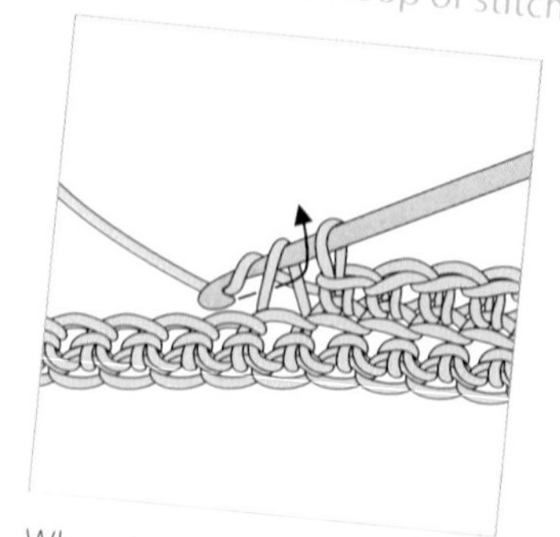

When inserting the hook into the stitch of the previous row or round, make sure it always only goes into the back loop of the stitch. Then continue working in the appropriate stitch (we are using single crochet/ UK double here).

Slip stitch

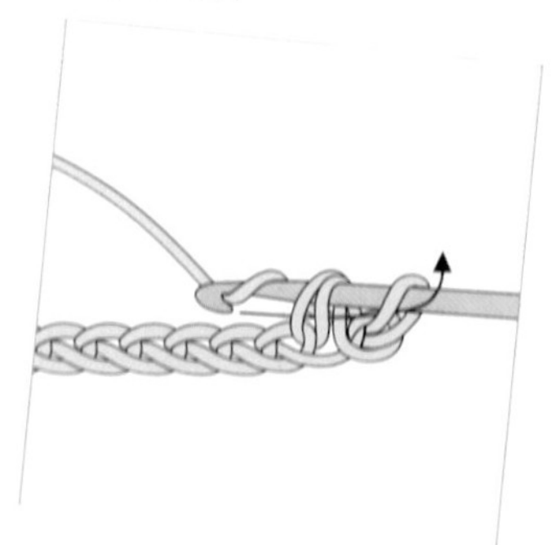

Insert hook in intended stitch, yarn over hook and pull through all the loops on the hook.

Double crochet (UK treble)

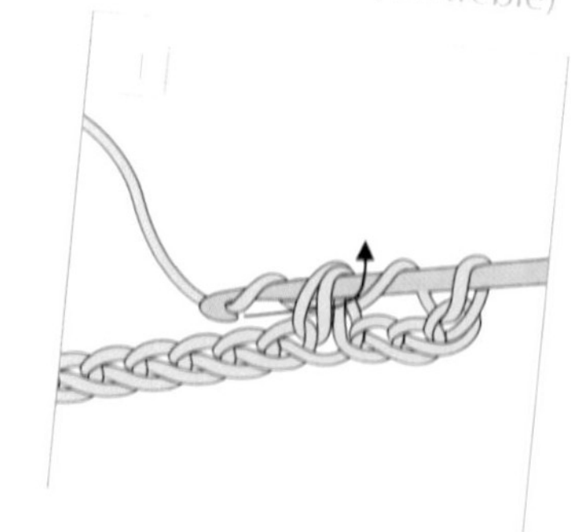

Yarn over hook and insert in intended stitch. Yarn over hook and draw through the stitch. Yarn over hook.

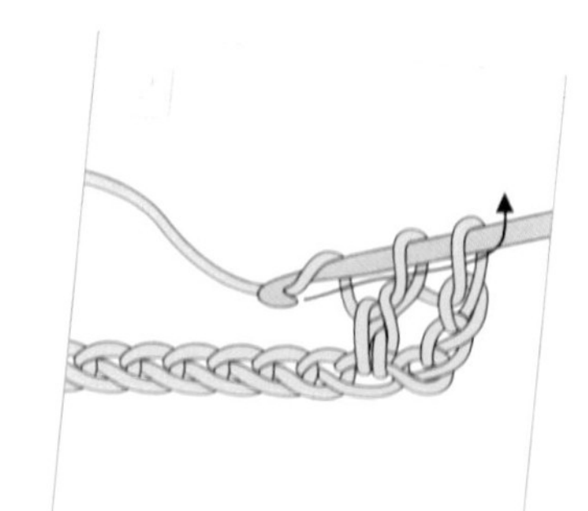

Draw yarn through first 2 loops on hook. Yarn over hook.

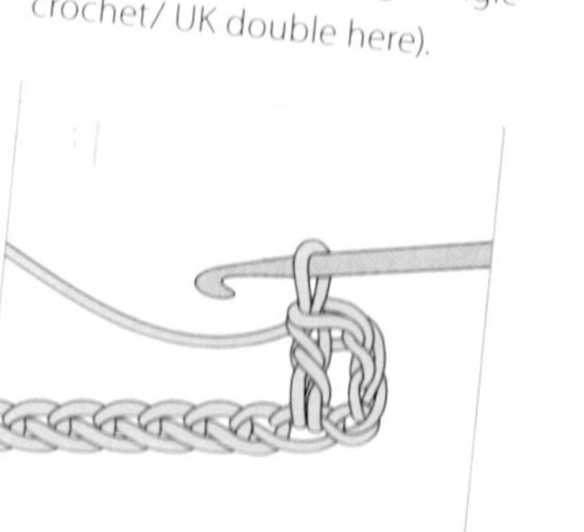

Draw yarn through remaining two loops. You have completed a double crochet (UK treble). Repeat as often as desired.

Half double crochet (UK half treble)

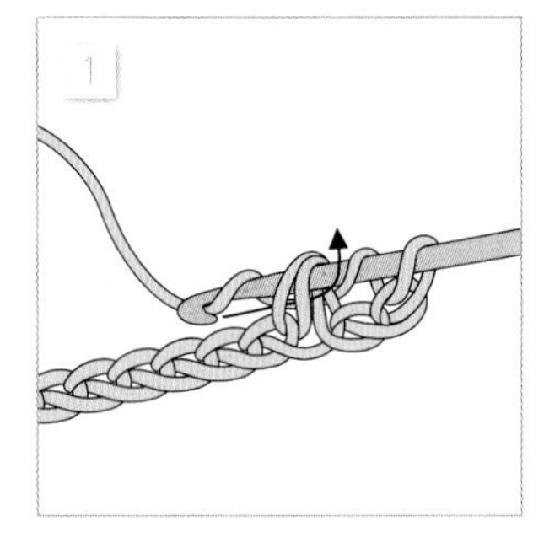

Yarn over hook and insert in intended stitch. Yarn over hook and draw through stitch.

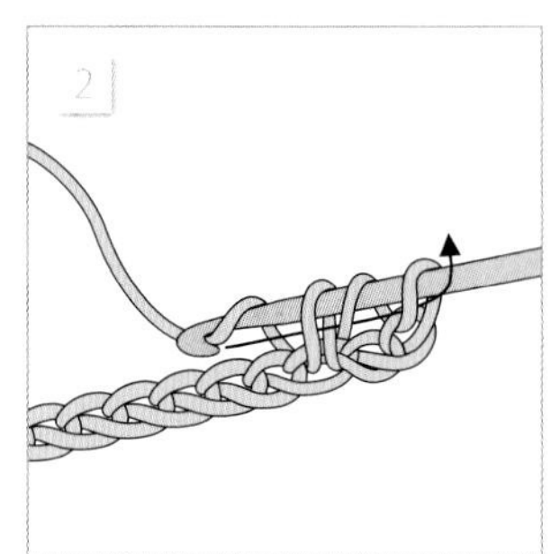

Yarn over hook and draw through all loops on hook. You have completed a half double crochet (UK half treble). Repeat as often as desired.

Treble crochet (UK double treble)

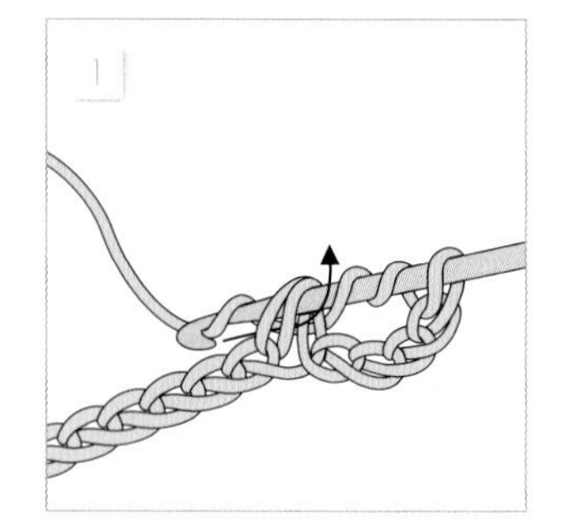

Yarn over hook twice and insert in intended stitch. Take up the yarn and draw through stitch. There should be 4 loops on the hook.

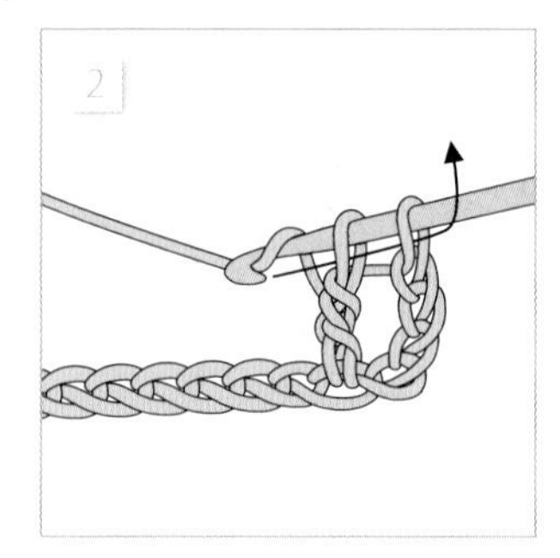

Yarn over hook and draw through first 2 loops. Yarn over hook and draw through next two loops. Yarn over hook and draw through last two loops. You have completed a treble crochet (UK double treble). Repeat as often as desired.

Relief double crochet (UK relief treble) from front

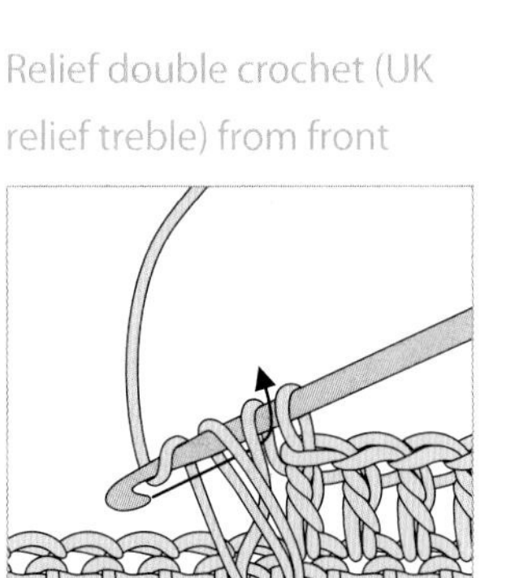

Yarn over hook, insert around double crochet (UK treble) in previous row from front to back, yarn over hook and draw through. Draw yarn through first two loops, then yarn over hook and draw through remaining two loops.

Relief double crochet (UK relief treble) from behind

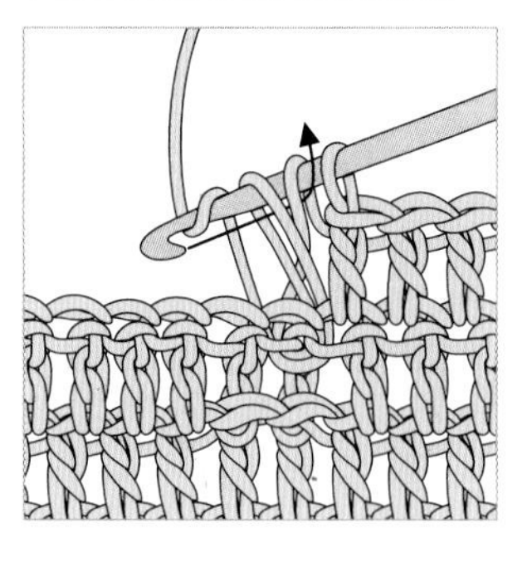

Yarn over hook, insert around double crochet (UK treble) in previous row from back to front, yarn over hook and draw through. Draw yarn through first two loops, then yarn over hook and draw through remaining two loops.

Picot edging or trim

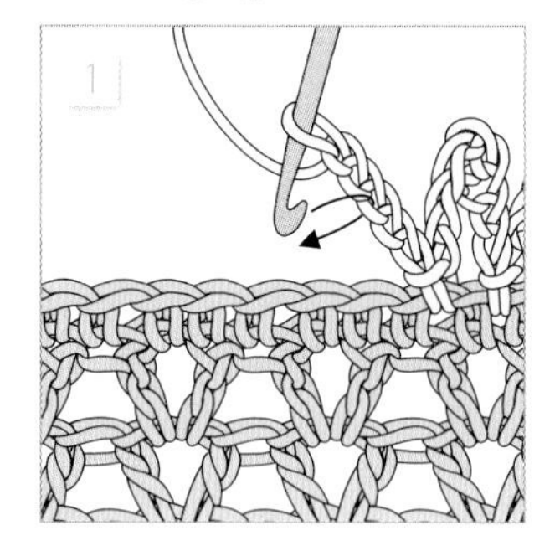

Slip stitch into first stitch of previous round. Now work *5 chain (or as stated in the pattern).

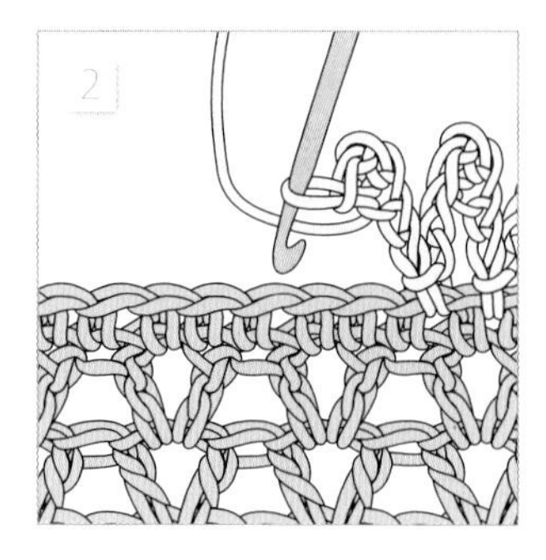

Then work one picot by crocheting 1 slip stitch into the third chain. 2 chain, then 1 slip stitch into the next stitch. Repeat from *.

Decrease: Double crochet (treble) 2 together

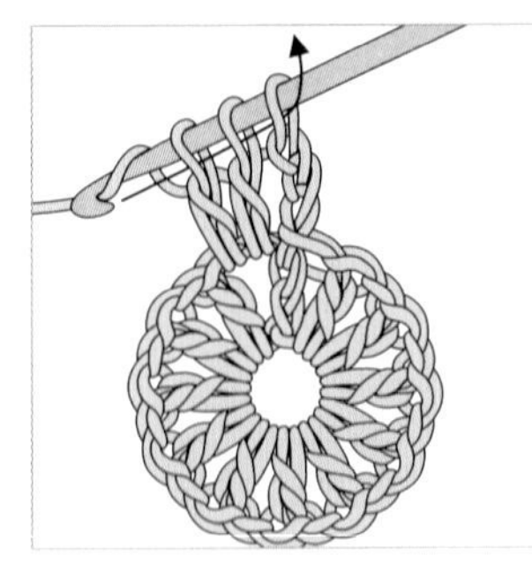

Work one double crochet (UK treble), but only draw yarn through 2 loops once. Then work the second double crochet (UK treble) as you did the first one. Yarn over hook and draw through all 3 loops.

Double crochet cluster (UK treble) in same stitch (puff or cluster stitch)

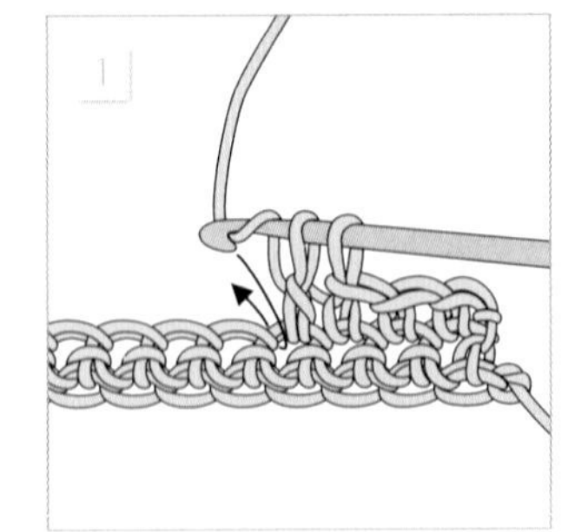

Work one double (UK treble) crochet until you have only 2 loops left on the hook.
Do not work these 2 loops as normal, but …

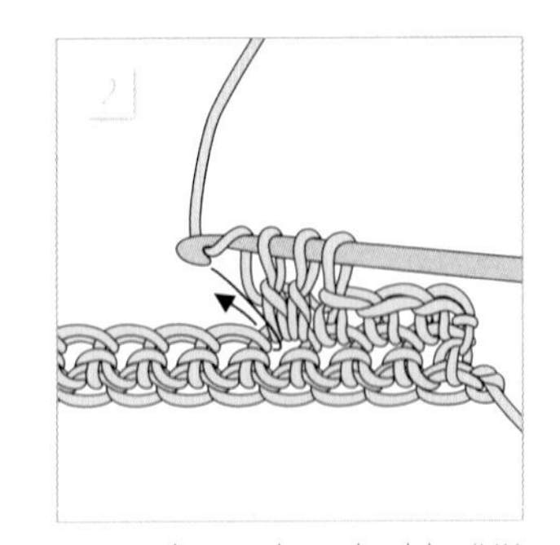

… work another double (UK treble) crochet into the same stitch without completing it.

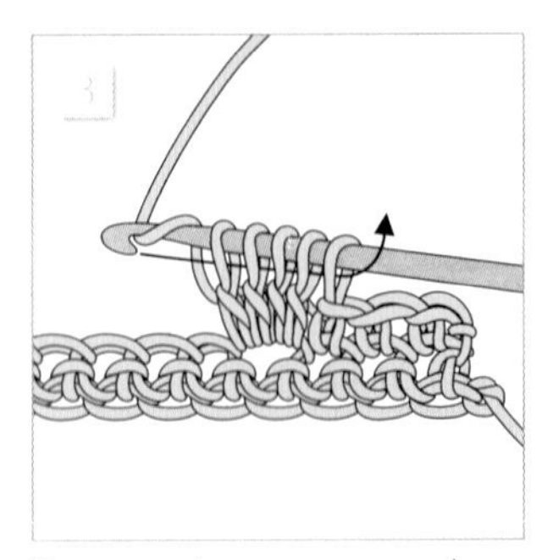

Repeat twice more so you have 5 loops on the hook and 4 double crochet (UK treble) cluster in one stitch. Yarn over hook and draw through all 5 loops on the hook. In other words finish (close) all 4 double crochet (UK treble) together.

Crochet in rounds

Crochet the required number of single (double) crochet into a ring of chain stitches or, as shown here, in a yarn loop. Join the round with 1 slip stitch into the first single (double) crochet.

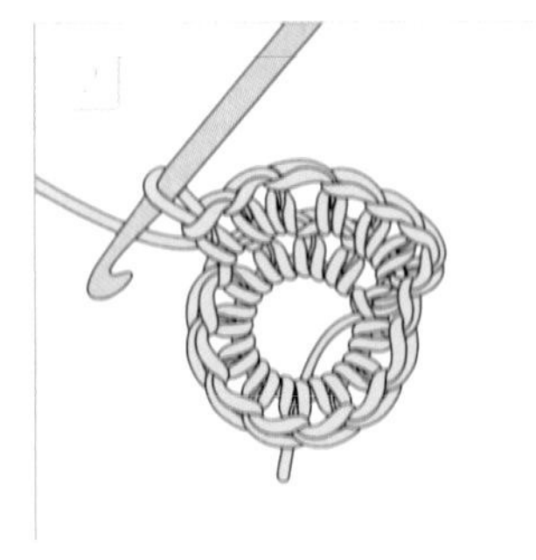

Start each round with the required number of chain stitches for the type of stitch. Increase each round as indicated in the pattern.

Joining yarn

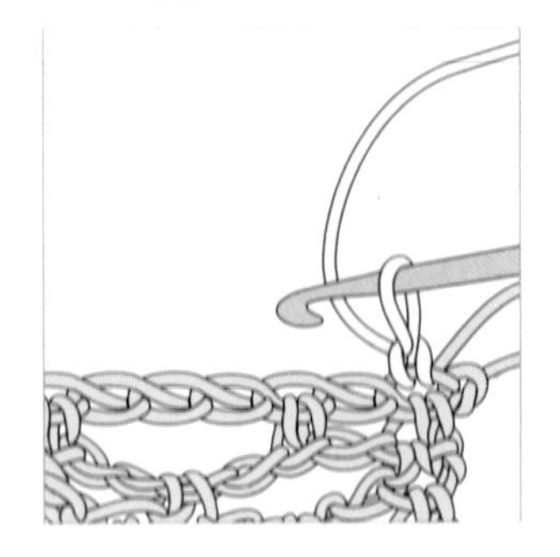

The yarn is behind your work. Insert hook as required, yarn over hook and draw through stitch. Yarn over hook and draw through loop (= slip stitch).

Changing colours

In order to achieve a precise changeover in colour when crocheting, you will often finish the last stitch in the previous round or row with the new colour. However, a different method is recommended for granny squares to make the changeover particularly clean: finish the round with 1 slip stitch in the old colour and weave in the end. Join the new colour at a slightly different place in the round with 1 slip stitch.

Spring

bright. breezy. beautiful.

Bracelet

fine. floral. fabulous.

Size: approximately 18.5cm (7¼in) circumference • Level of difficulty *

Materials

- Cotton yarn (100% cotton, length 125m/50g, 136¾yd/1¼oz): 50g (1¼oz) each in olive, yellow and green
- Crochet hook no. 1/B or C US (2.5mm)
- 2 buttons

Gauge

1 crocheted square = 4.5 x 4.5cm (1¾ x 1¾in)

Colour sequence of the cuff

Circle of chain and Round 1: Olive

Round 2: Yellow

Round 3: Green

Slip stitch and crochet: Green

How it's done

To crochet a square, crochet 6 chain into a ring and work Rounds 1-3 of Pattern 1. After that, change the colour for every round (see colour sequence), joining each new colour with a slip stitch (see pattern 1). Work four squares in the colours of your choice for each cuff. Join the squares together with slip stitches to make a strip.

Then crochet along both long sides of the cuff. On one short side, work loops in chain stitch for the buttons as shown in pattern 2. Work the single crochet (UK double) into the back loop of the stitch only. Sew on the buttons.

Crochet pattern 1

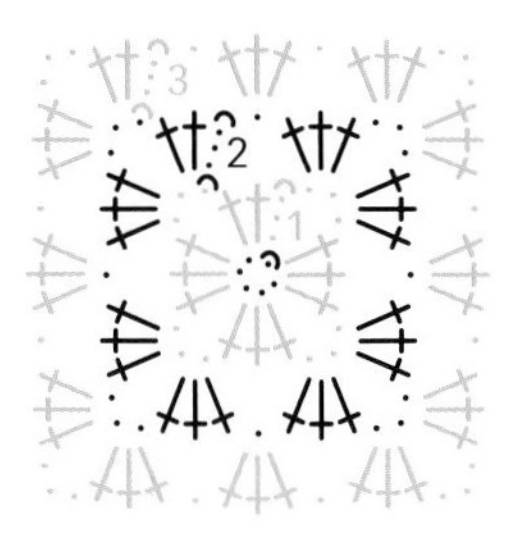

Symbols

- . = 1 chain
- ⌒ = 1 slip stitch
- I = 1 single crochet (UK double)
- † = 1 double crochet (UK treble)

Diagram with crochet pattern 2

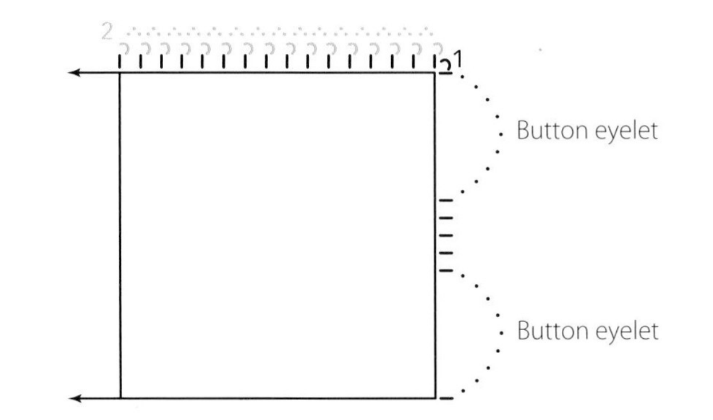

Phone case

cheerful. cool. charming.

Size: 15 x 7.5cm (6 x 3in) • Level of difficulty ***

Materials

- Mixed cotton yarn (97% cotton, 3% polyester, length approximately 125m/50g, 136¾yd/1¼oz): 50g (1¼oz) each in light blue, soft green, blue, May green, lilac, pale yellow, vanilla yellow and silver grey
- Crochet hook no. 7 US (4.5mm)

Gauge

1 crocheted square = 7 x 7cm (2¾in)

Crochet pattern

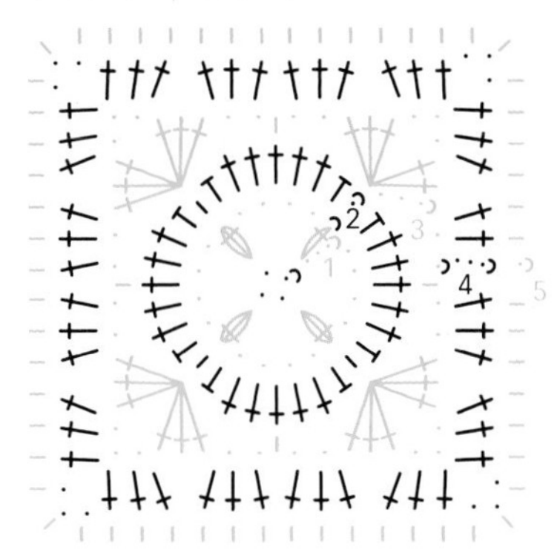

Symbols

- · = 1 chain
- ⌒ = 1 slip stitch
- I = 1 single crochet (UK double)
- T = 1 half double crochet (UK half treble)
- † = 1 double crochet (UK treble)
- = half-closed 3 double crochet (UK treble) in same stitch
- = half-closed 2 double crochet (UK treble) in same stitch

How it's done

To crochet a square, crochet 4 chain into a ring and work Rounds 1–5 of the pattern. Change the colour at the end of each round, only working Rounds 4 and 5 in the same colour. Join each new colour with a slip stitch (see pattern).

Work four squares in total, using a different sequence of colours for each, to make one phone case. Sew up the ends, and crochet two squares together (right sides facing) on one side using slip stitch.

Then place both pieces together with the wrong sides facing, and crochet together on three sides using picot stitch (see Basic crochet course, page 10).

Leave open at the top.

Pencil case

practical. pastel. perfect.

Size: approximately 9.5 x 25cm (3¾ x 9¾in) • Level of difficulty ✻✻✻

Materials

- Cotton yarn (100% cotton, length 75m/50g, 82yd/1¾oz): 100g (3½oz) in natural, 50g (1¾oz) each in lilac, lime green, yellow and blue
- Crochet hook no. 7 US (4.5mm)
- Zip in white or other matching colour, 24cm (9½in)
- Sewing thread in a matching colour, sewing needle

Gauge

1 crocheted square = 7.5 x 7.5cm (3 x 3in)

Colour sequence

Circle of chain and Round 1: Lilac, blue or lime green

Round 2: Yellow

Round 3: Natural

Slip stitch and trebles to finish: Natural

How it's done

To crochet a square, crochet 4 chain into a ring and work Rounds 1–3 of the pattern. After that, change the colour for every round (see colour sequence), joining each new colour with a slip stitch (see pattern).

Work a total of six squares, and join them together in threes using slip stitches. Work 1 round of double crochet (UK treble) around these pieces in natural, working 3 double crochet (UK treble) into the corner stitches.

Join the two pieces together with slip stitches in natural. Sew a zip into the top opening by hand. Make a small loop in lime green. Crochet 7 chain, then work 1 row of single crochet (UK double) into them. Attach the loop to the eyelet of the zip.

Symbols

- · = 1 chain
- ⌒ = 1 slip stitch
- † = 1 double crochet (UK treble)
- = 4 double crochet cluster (UK treble) in same stitch
- = 3 double crochet cluster (UK treble) in same stitch

Crochet pattern

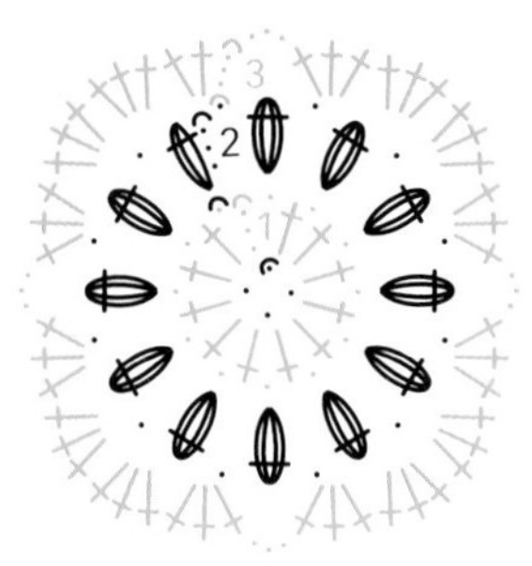

Doilie wraps

graceful. glossy. geometric.

Size: approximately 26 x 6cm (10¼ x 2½in) wide

Level of difficulty ***

Materials

- Silk yarn with linen (80% silk, 20% linen, length approximately 150m/50g, 164yd/1¾oz): 50g (1¾oz) each in green, orange, taupe and grey
- Crochet hook no. 00 US (3mm)

Gauge

1 crocheted square = 6 x 6cm (2½ x 2½in)

Crochet pattern

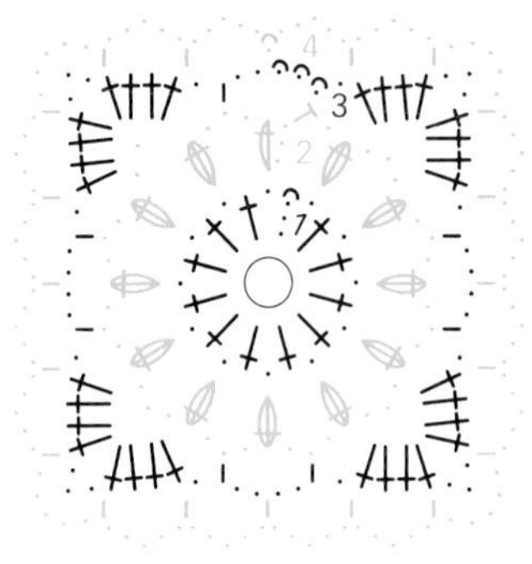

Symbols

· = 1 chain

⌒ = 1 slip stitch

I = 1 single crochet (UK double)

T = 1 half double crochet (UK half treble)

† = 1 double crochet (UK treble)

= 3 double crochet cluster (UK treble) in same stitch

= 2 double crochet cluster (UK treble) in same stitch

How it's done

To make a square, create a magic ring using a double loop (see page 8) and work Rounds 1–4 of the pattern.

Work four squares in the colour of your choice to fit the glass, and then crochet them together with slip stitches. Sew in the threads. Work 4 rows of chain stitches for each cover and sew onto the ends of the squares. Place around a glass and tie together with two lengths of chain.

Shawl

floaty. fine. fairy-like.

Size: 75 x 150cm (29½ x 59in) • Level of difficulty ✳✳✳✳✳

Materials

- Cotton blend with silk and cashmere (85% cotton, 10% silk, 5% cashmere, length 95m/50g, 104yd/1¾oz): 450g (16oz) in stone
- Crochet hook no. 6 US (4mm)

Gauge

1 crochet motif = 11.5 x 11.5cm (4½ x 4½in)

Crochet pattern 2

Crochet pattern 3

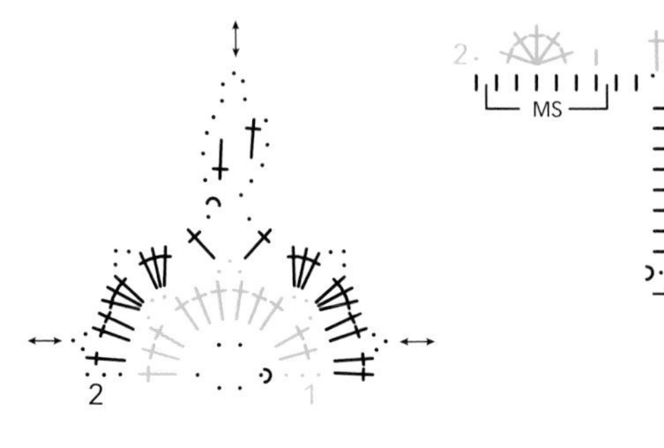

Crochet pattern 1

Symbols

· = 1 chain

◠ = 1 slip stitch

ı = 1 single crochet (UK double)

† = 1 double crochet (UK treble)

If the symbols are joined at the bottom, the stitches are worked into the same stitch of the previous round.

↔ = Join = When crocheting the chain loop, work through the chain loop of the neighbouring motif to join.

How it's done

To make a whole motif, create a magic ring using a double loop (see page 8) and work Rounds 1–5 of pattern 1. For a half motif, crochet 6 chain into a ring and work Rows 1 and 2 of pattern 2.

Crochet a motif, and when crocheting the chain loop of the last round of the second motif, link it to the first motif (see pattern 1). Work all the motifs in this way and join together as indicated in the diagram. A total of 36 whole motifs and 10 half motifs are required.

Work 1 round of single crochet (UK double) all around the finished shawl (see pattern 3), starting at the first short side (right) and working 2 chain between 2 single crochet (UK double) in the corners. Start the round with 1 chain (counts as the first single crochet /UK double) and close with 1 slip stitch. Now work 1 chain and finish the two shorts sides with a row of shell trim as indicated in pattern 3. Close with 1 slip stitch.

Diagram

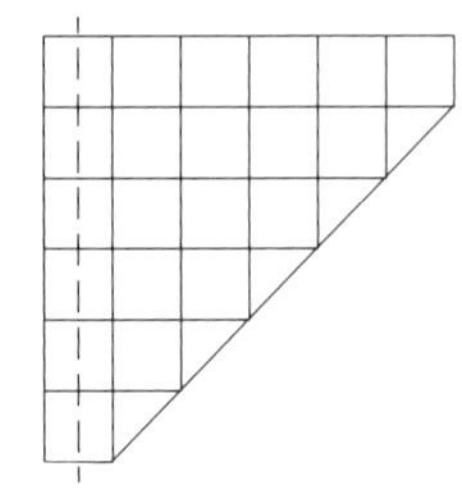

Mirror image here

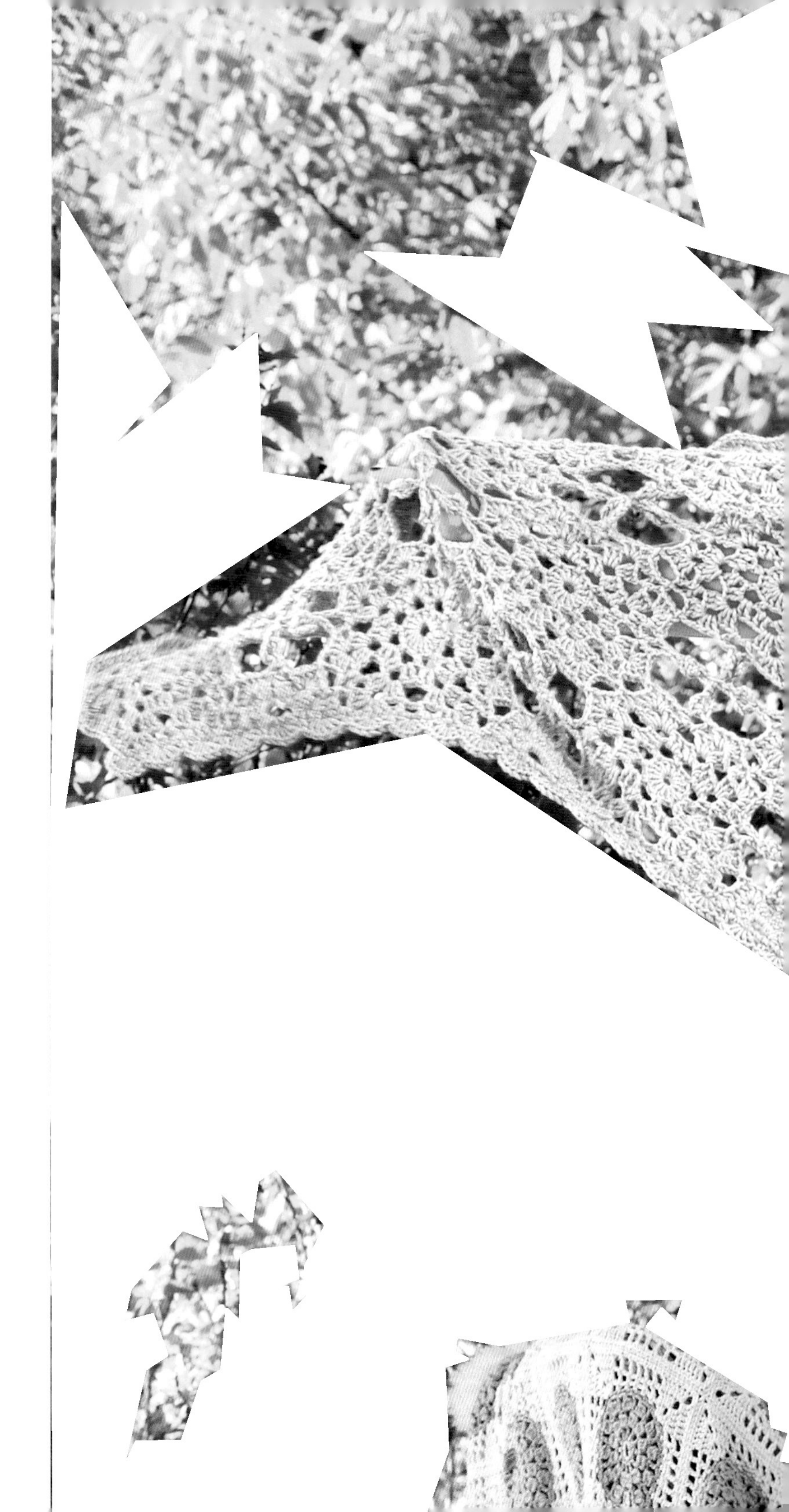

Throw

soft. stylish. silky.

Size: 125 x 165cm (49¼ x 65in) • Level of difficulty ****

Materials

- Silk yarn (100% silk, length 120m/50g, 131¼yd/1¾oz): 1100g (39oz) in cream, 250g (9oz) each in pale pink, grey blue and taupe
- Crochet hook no. 6 US (4mm)

Gauge

1 crocheted square = 13 x 13cm (5 x 5in)

Colour sequence of square

Rounds 1–5 : Pale pink or grey blue or taupe

Rounds 6–9 : Cream

How it's done

To make a square, create a magic ring using a double loop (see page 8) and work Rounds 1–9 of pattern 1 in the sequence of colours indicated. Make a total of 108 squares. Slip stitch the squares together in nine rows of 12 squares in the cream yarn.

Crochet a border around the throw to Pattern 2. A pattern is worked over 4 stitches; continue repeating this pattern. Work the corners as indicated in the pattern.

Crochet pattern 1

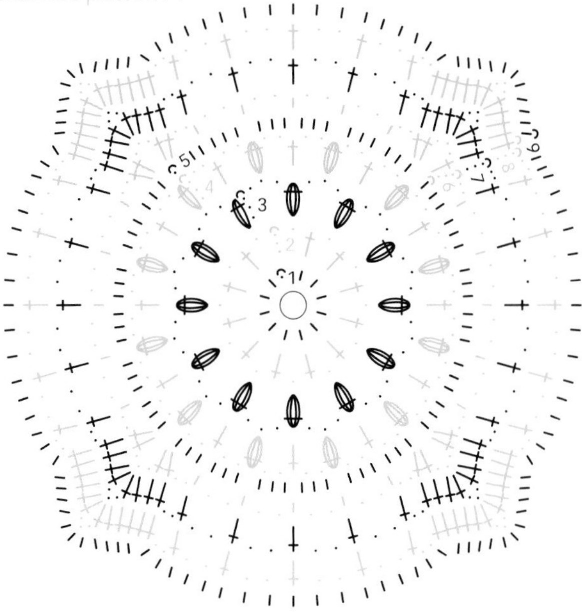

Crochet pattern 2

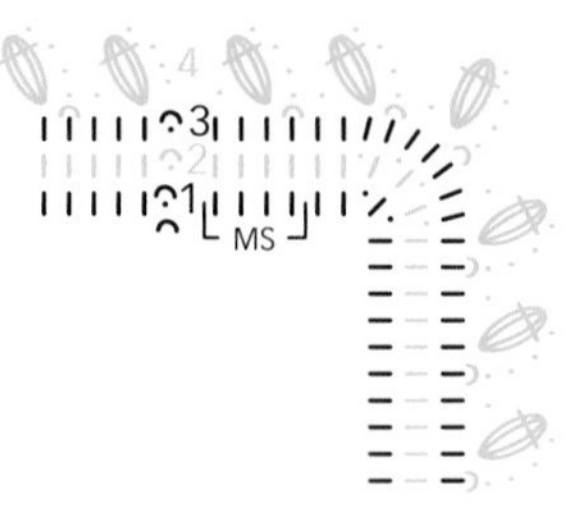

Symbols

· = 1 chain

⌒ = 1 slip stitch

I = 1 single crochet (UK double)

† = 1 double crochet (UK treble)

= 3 double crochet cluster (UK treble) in same stitch

= 4 double crochet cluster (UK treble) in same stitch

Summer

fresh. fabulous. free.

White tablecloth

neat. nostalgic. natural.

Size: approximately 120 x 160cm (47¼ x 63in) • Level of difficulty *****

Materials

- Mixed cotton yarn (60% cotton, 40% modal, length approximately 100m/50g, 109¼in/1¾oz): 1750g (61¾oz) in white
- Crochet hook no. 8/H US (5mm)

Gauge

1 crocheted square = 15 x 15cm (6 x 6in)

How it's done

To make a square, create a magic ring using a double loop (see page 8) and work Rounds 1–8 of pattern 1. Make a total of 96 squares. Weave in all the threads and slip stitch the squares together. The tablecloth is eight squares wide and 12 squares long.

Crochet a border around the tablecloth to pattern 2. A pattern repeat is worked over 6 stitches, and the repeat is crocheted five times per square. Work the corners as indicated in the pattern.

Crochet pattern 1

Crochet pattern 2

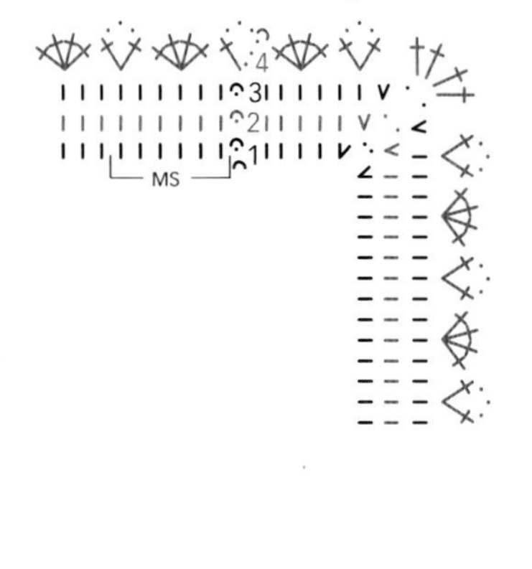

Symbols

- · = 1 chain
- ⌒ = 1 slip stitch
- I = 1 single crochet (UK double)
- † = 1 double crochet (UK treble)

Flower curtain

cute. comical. creative.

Size: approximately 120 x 160cm (47¼ x 63in) · Level of difficulty ✱✱

Materials

- Cotton yarn (100% cotton, combed, length 80m/50g, 87½yd/1¾oz): 100g (3½oz) green, 50g (1¾oz) each in red, blue, dark orange, orange, light orange, yellow, lilac, lavender, bright pink and turquoise
- Crochet hook no. 8/H US (5mm)
- 1 round wooden bar of the desired length (width of door or window)

Gauge

1 crocheted flower = 5cm (2in) diameter

Crochet Pattern 1

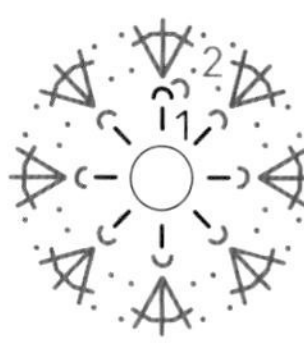

Crochet Pattern 2

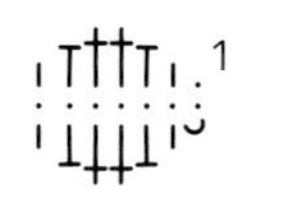

Symbols

- · = 1 chain
- ⌒ = 1 slip stitch
- ı = 1 single crochet (UK double)
- T = 1 half double crochet (UK half treble)
- † = 1 double crochet (UK treble)

How it's done

To crochet a flower, work Rounds 1 and 2 of pattern 1 into a loop. Choose the colours in any sequence, and change the colour after Round 1. Work the desired number of green leaves to pattern 2. Work as many flowers and leaves as you like.

Now work long ropes of chain stitches in green. Make the length to suit the door or window where you want to hang the curtain.

Then crochet on flowers and leaves in turn.

Finish by making a line of chains the length of the piece of wood and work 1 row of single crochet (UK double). Work as many rows of single crochet (UK double) as required to cover the wooden bar, and then sew it over the bar.

Stole

exclusive. elegant. exquisite.

Size: approximately 35 x 180cm (13¾ x 71in) · Level of difficulty ***

Materials

- Viscose yarn (80% bamboo viscose, 20% merino wool, length 100m/50g, 109½yd/1¾oz): 450g (16oz) red, 300g (10½oz) pale pink and 250g (9oz) pink
- Crochet hook no. 6 US (4mm)

Gauge

1 crocheted square = approximately 5 x 5cm (2 x 2in)

Colour sequence of square

Round 1: Red

Round 2: Pale pink

Round 3: Pink

Round 4: Red

How it's done

To make a square, create a magic ring using a double loop (see page 8) and work Rounds 1–4 of pattern 1 in the sequence of colours indicated. Make a total of 135 squares as indicated in the pattern. Slip stitch the squares together, making 27 rows of five squares.

Now crochet a border around the stole in red to pattern 2: a pattern repeat is worked over 6 stitches, and the repeat is crocheted 5 times per square. Work the corners as indicated in the pattern.

Secure all the threads and press the stole under a damp cloth to finish.

Crochet pattern 1

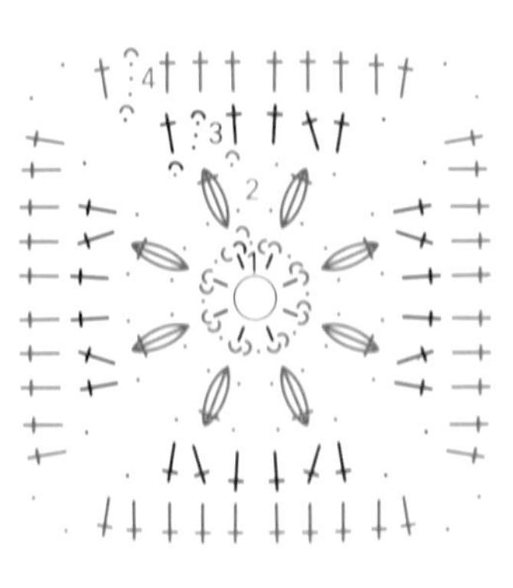

Crochet pattern 2

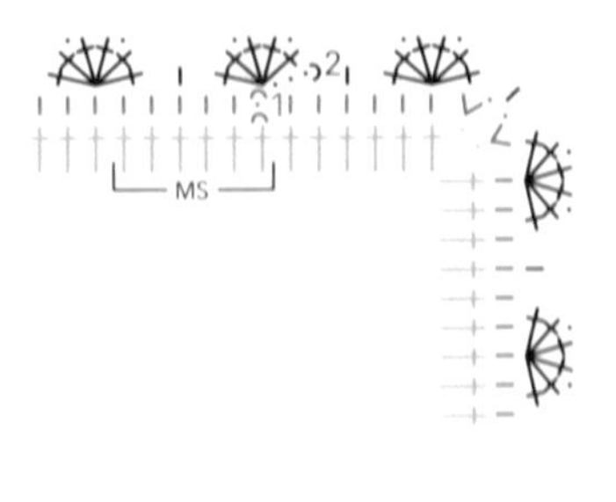

Symbols

- · = 1 chain
- ⌒ = 1 slip stitch
- ı = 1 single crochet (UK double)
- † = 1 double crochet (UK treble)
- ⬯ = 3 double crochet cluster (UK treble) in same stitch

Shopping bag

big. bountiful. bright.

Size: 40 x 33cm, (15¾ x 13in) high • Level of difficulty **

Materials

- Cotton yarn (100% cotton, length 125m/50g, 136¾yd/1¾oz): 400g (14oz) turquoise, 100g (3½oz) each in orange, pale pink, yellow and green
- Crochet hook no. 00 US (3mm)

Gauge

1 crocheted square = approximately 4.5 x 4.5cm (1¾ x 1¾in)

Crochet pattern

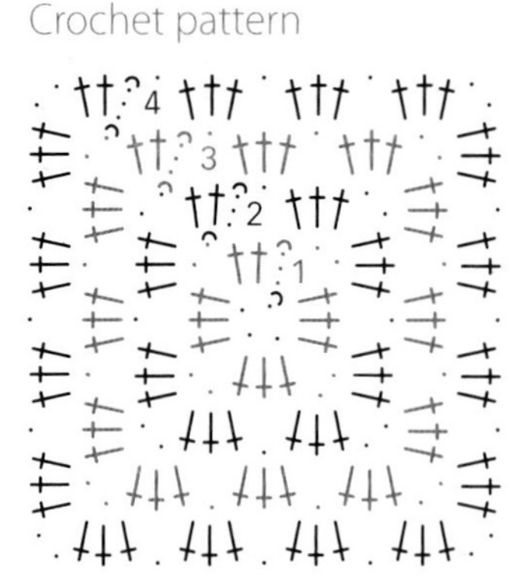

Symbols

- • = 1 chain
- ⌒ = 1 slip stitch
- † = 1 double crochet (UK treble)

How it's done

To make a square, crochet 4 chain into a ring and work Rounds 1–4 of the pattern. Change the colour in every round, joining each new colour with 1 slip stitch (see pattern). Make a total of 64 squares in different colour sequences, but always work Round 4 in turquoise. Crochet the squares together using slip stitch as shown in the diagram. Sew in the threads. To make the handles, work the desired length of chain stitches in turquoise and then crochet rows of single crochet (UK double) as follows, turning at the end with 1 chain:

Row 1: Turquoise
Row 2: Pale pink
Row 3: Yellow
Row 4: Green
Row 5: Orange
Row 6: Green
Row 7: Yellow
Row 8: Pale pink
Row 9: Turquoise

Weave in the threads and sew both handles to the bag.

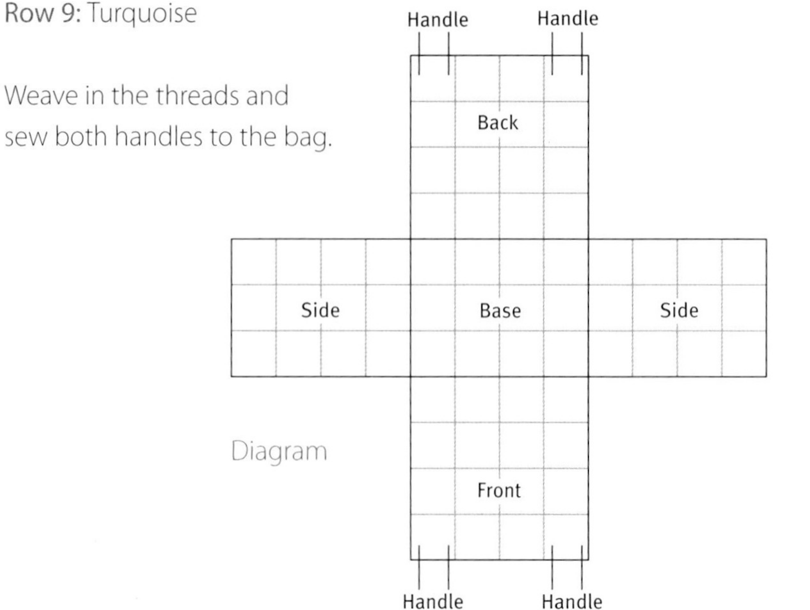

Diagram

Bench pillow

lazy. laid-back. lovely.

Size: approximately 55 x 35cm (21¾ x 13¾in) • Level of difficulty ✻✻✻

Materials

- Cotton yarn (100% cotton, combed, length approx. 80m/50g, 87½yd/1¾oz): 700g (24½oz) white (main colour of crocheted squares and back), 50g (1¾oz) each red, pale yellow, yellow, orange and pale pink or yellow, blue, light blue, turquoise and green (colours for the middle of the squares)
- Crochet hook no. 6 US (4mm)
- 3 or 4 white buttons

Gauge

1 crocheted square = 8 x 8cm (3¼ x 3¼in)

Colour sequence of square

Chain ring and Round 1: One colour for the middle

Rounds 2–4: White

How it's done

To make a square, crochet 4 chain into a ring and work Rounds 1–4 of the pattern. Make a total of 24 squares (see colour sequence). Crochet the squares together in four rows of six squares, taking care not to place any squares with middles that are the same colour together.
For one back piece, crochet 96 chain + 3 turning chain and work rows of double crochet (UK treble). Turn each row with 3 chain.
Finish after 26 rows. Repeat for the second back piece, but working buttonholes in the bottom. Crochet as far as the desired position of the buttonhole, and then work enough chain stitches over the double crochet (UK treble) to cover the size of the buttonhole. Secure the chain stitches with a double crochet (UK treble) into the next stitch.
Work the next buttonholes in the same way. In the next row, work one stitch into each of the chain stitches in the previous row. Crochet the two back pieces together with the fronts overlapping. Sew on the buttons.

Crochet pattern

Symbols

- · = 1 chain
- ⌒ = 1 slip stitch
- † = 1 double crochet (UK treble)
- = 5 double crochet cluster (UK treble) in same stitch
- = 4 double crochet cluster (UK treble) in same stitch

Autumn

colourful. comfortable. cosy.

Poncho

soft. slinky. smooth.

Size: approximately 88 x 100cm (34¾ x 39½in) • Level of difficulty ✶✶

Materials

- Alpaca wool (100% alpaca, length 85m/50g, 93yd/1¾oz): 250g (9oz) each in silver grey, natural, brown and silky grey
- Crochet hook no. 7 US (4.5mm)

Gauge

1 crocheted square = approximately 8 x 8cm (3¼ x 3¼in)

How it's done

To make a square, create a magic ring using a double loop (see page 8) and work Rounds 1–3 of the pattern. Change the colour after every round, joining each new colour with 1 slip stitch (see pattern).

Make a total of 132 squares in as many different colour combinations as you can.

Then sew the squares together as shown in the diagram. Work 2 rows of single crochet (UK double) along the top and bottom in brown as the border.

Crochet pattern

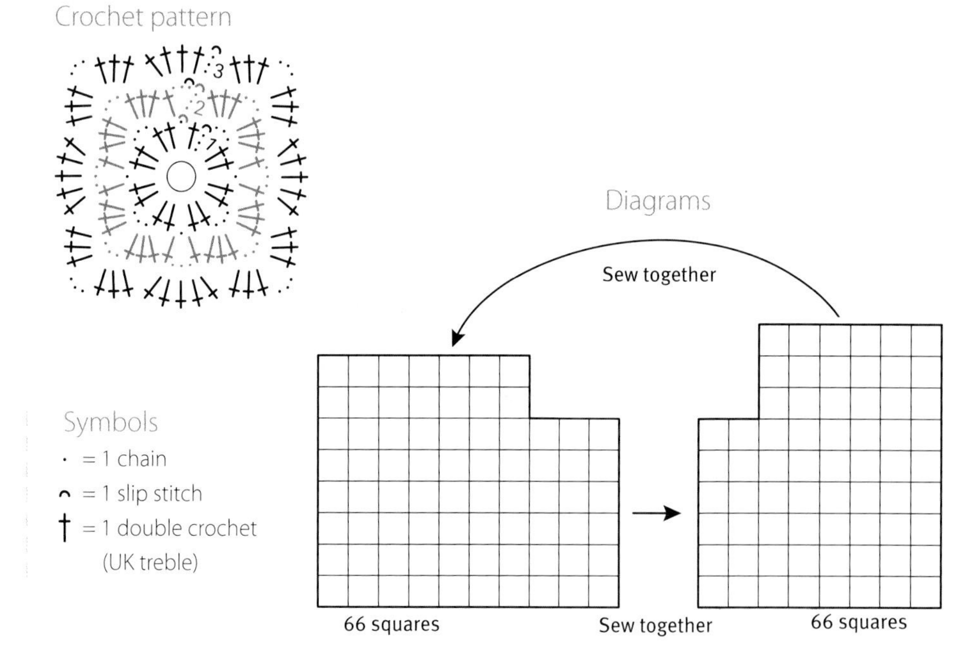

Symbols

· = 1 chain

⌒ = 1 slip stitch

† = 1 double crochet (UK treble)

Retro miniskirt

iconic. irrestistible. individual.

Size: UK 10/12 (US 8/10, EU 36/38 , Medium) • Level of difficulty ✲✲

Materials

- Wool/silk blend (70% new wool, 20% silk, 10% cashmere, length 115m/50 g, 125¾yd/1¾oz): 150g (5¼oz) olive, 100g (3½oz) each in brown, light green and mustard, 50g (1¾oz) each in grey and black
- Crochet hook no. 6 US (4mm)

Gauge

1 crocheted square = approximately 13 x 13cm (5 x 5in)

Colour sequence of square

Circle of chain and Round 1: Mustard

Round 1: Black
Round 3: Grey
Round 4: Brown
Round 5: Mustard
Round 6: Light green
Round 7: Olive

Crochet pattern

How it's done

To make a square, crochet 4 chain into a ring and work Rounds 1–7 of the pattern. Work in the sequence of colours shown, joining each new colour with 1 slip stitch (see pattern). Work a total of 24 squares in this colour sequence.

Slip stitch the squares together in olive yarn: three squares in height and four in width for the front and back of the skirt (see photo). Then join the two pieces together, again with slip stitches in olive.

To make the waistband, work 7 rounds of double crochet (UK trebles) in olive along the top edge, with decreases. Work 3 chain at the beginning of each round to replace the first double crochet (UK treble), and end each round with 1 slip stitch.

Round 1: 1 double crochet (UK treble) in each stitch.

Round 2–3: Work in double crochet (UK treble), missing every fourth stitch.

Round 4–7: Work in double crochet (UK treble), missing every eighth stitch. Work 1 row of double crochet (UK treble) along the bottom edge in olive.

Symbols

- · = 1 chain
- ⌒ = 1 slip stitch
- † = 1 double crochet (UK treble)

Brooch

soft. silky. stunning.

Size: 6cm (2½in) diameter · Level of difficulty *

Materials

To make one brooch

- Alpaca wool (100% alpaca, length 85m/50g, 93yd/1¾oz): 50g (1¾oz) each in cream and silver-grey
- Crochet hook no. 7 US (4.5mm)
- 1 button in a matching colour
- Fabric scrap in a matching colour
- Brooch

Gauge

1 crocheted flower = 6cm (2½in) diameter

Crochet pattern

Symbols

- · = 1 chain
- ⌒ = 1 slip stitch
- ı = 1 single crochet (UK double)
- T = 1 half double crochet (UK half treble)
- † = 1 double crochet (UK treble)
- ⏀ = 3 double crochet cluster (UK treble) in same stitch

How it's done

To make a flower, create a magic ring using a double loop (see page 8) and work Rounds 1–4 of the pattern. Crochet a flower to the pattern for each brooch, and weave in the threads. Sew a button to the middle of the flower. Sew the flower onto a circle of fabric and attach a brooch pin to the back.

Throw

masculine. marvellous. memorable.

Size: approximately 135 x 180cm (53½ x 71in) • Level of difficulty ✶✶

Materials

- Wool blend (50% new wool, 25% alpaca, 25% polyamide, length 55m/50g, 60yd/1¾oz): 850g (30oz) grey, 500g (17½oz) olive grey and 400g (14oz) light grey (main colours of crochet squares and trim), scraps in chestnut, rust, wine red, moss, khaki, dusky pink, navy, denim, petrol, black-lilac and anthracite (colours for the middles of the crochet squares)
- Crochet hook no. 15/N US (9mm)

Gauge

1 crocheted square = 21 x 21cm (8¼ x 8¼in)

Colour sequence of square

Round 1: One colour for the middle

Round 2: Light grey

Round 3: Olive grey

Round 4: Grey

Symbols

• = 1 chain

⌒ = 1 slip stitch

† = 1 double crochet (UK treble)

How it's done

To make a square, create a magic ring using a double loop (see page 8) and work Rounds 1–4 of the pattern. Work a total of 48 squares in the colour sequence shown, making sure the colours for the middles are all different.

Weave in the threads and slip stitch the squares together: 8 rows of 6 squares.

Now work 2 rounds of single crochet (UK double) in grey around the throw. Only work into the back loop of each stitch, and start Round 2 with 1 chain to replace the first single crochet (UK double). Finish the rounds with 1 slip stitch. Always work 3 single crochet (UK double) into 1 stitch at the corners. Now work 3 rounds of half double crochet (UK half treble). Work Round 1 in light grey, Round 2 in olive grey and Round 3 in grey. Work 2 chain at the beginning of each round to replace the first half double crochet (UK half treble), and finish each round with 1 slip stitch. Always work 3 half double crochet (UK treble) into 1 stitch at the corners.

Crochet pattern

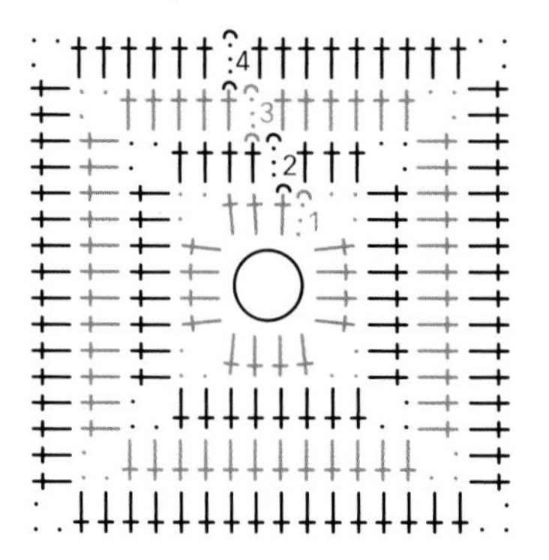

Satchel

fresh. friendly. fab.

Size: 35 x 27cm (13¾ x 10¾in) • Level of difficulty ✱✱

Materials

- Cotton yarn with wool (70% cotton, 30% new wool, length 85m/50g, 93yd/1¾oz): 300g (10½oz) anthracite, 50g (1¾oz) each in natural, black, chestnut, silver-grey and navy
- Crochet hook no. 7 US (4.5mm)
- Buckle, approximately 6cm (2½in)

Gauge

1 crocheted square = 7.5 x 7.5cm (3 x 3in)

Crochet pattern

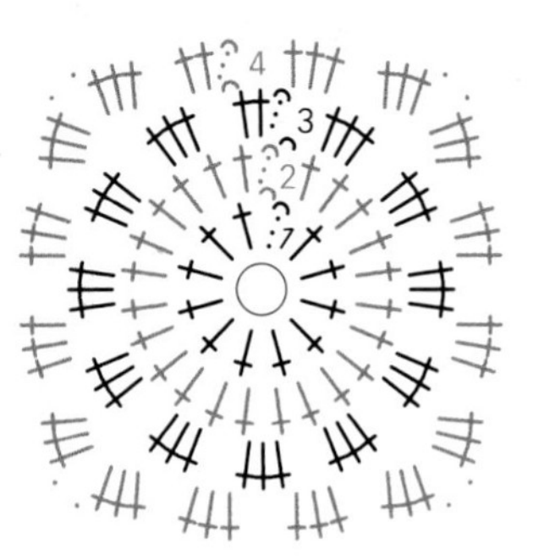

Symbols

· = 1 chain

ᴖ = 1 slip stitch

† = 1 double crochet (UK treble)

How it's done

To make a square, create a magic ring using a double loop (see page 8) and work Rounds 1–4 of the pattern. Make a total of 36 squares in different colour sequences. Change the colour after each round, but always work Round 4 in anthracite. Join each new colour with 1 slip stitch (see pattern).

Slip stitch the squares together to make the front (12 squares) and the back with the flap (24 squares).

For the strap with the bag sides and base, crochet 10 chain and work in rows as follows: *turn, 2 chain, 9 half double crochet (UK half treble). Repeat from * until the strap measures about 210cm (83in).

Place the strap against the three sides of the back of the bag so it overlaps slightly on the left. Slip stitch both pieces together. Slip stitch the front onto the bag.

Connect the two open pieces of the strap with a buckle.

Diagram

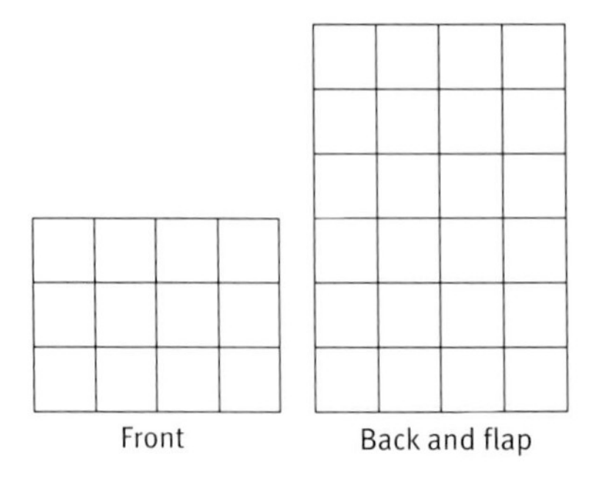

Winte
XMAS

hearty. homely. hip.

Granny square box

practical. pretty. perfect.

Size: 40 x 40cm (15¾ x 15¾in) • Level of difficulty ✱✱

Materials

- Alpaca wool (100% alpaca, length 85m/50g, 93yd/1¾oz): 800g (28¼oz) natural, 200g (7oz) each in black, anthracite, silver-grey, chestnut, khaki, curry and bordeaux
- Crochet hook no. 7 US (4.5mm)
- 1 foam cube, 40 x 40cm (15¾ x 15¾in)

Gauge

1 crocheted square = approximately 12.5 x 12.5cm (5 x 5in)

How it's done

To make a square, crochet 4 chain into a ring and work Rounds 1–4 of the pattern. Change the colour after every round, joining each new colour with 1 slip stitch (see pattern). Make a total of 54 squares in different colour sequences, but always work Round 4 in natural.
Slip stitch nine squares together. If you like, cover the foam cube in fabric.
Crochet the six resulting large squares (the sides of the cube) together and place over the foam cube, leaving one side open. Then either sew this side up or put in a zip as desired.

Crochet pattern

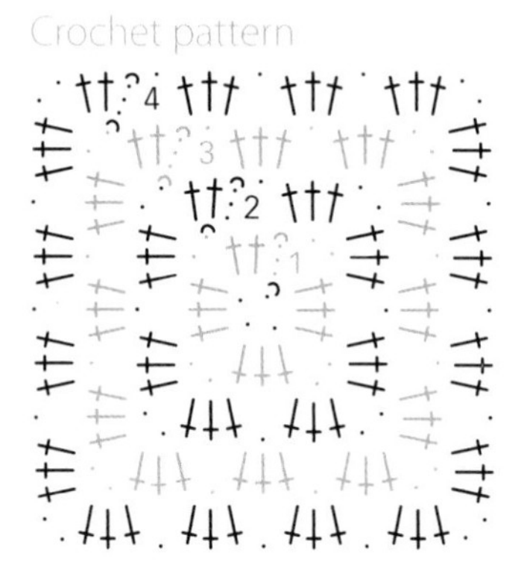

Symbols

· = 1 chain

⌒ = 1 slip stitch

† = 1 double crochet (UK treble)

Mohair scarf

sensous. soft. special.

Size: 185cm (73in) long • Level of difficulty ***

Materials

- Mohair yarn with silk (77% mohair, 23% silk, length approximately 175m/25g, 191½yd/¾oz): 25g (¾oz) each in light grey, red, dark grey and cream
- Crochet hook no. 6 US (4mm)

Gauge

1 crocheted flower = 9cm (3½in) diameter

Colour sequence of flower

Rounds 1–2: Red

Rounds 3–4: Change alternately to two of the remaining three colours (light grey, dark grey, cream)

Symbols

ᴖ = 1 chain

· = 1 slip stitch

ı = 1 single crochet (UK double)

† = 1 double crochet (UK treble)

= 2 double crochet cluster (UK treble) in same stitch

= 3 double crochet cluster (UK treble) in same stitch

Crochet pattern

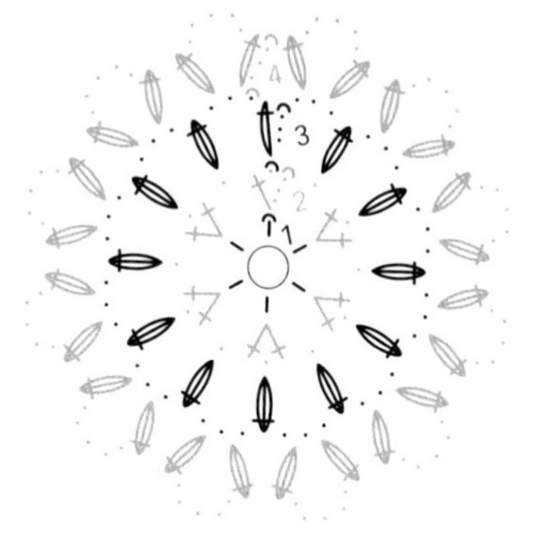

How it's done

To crochet a flower, create a magic ring using a double loop (see page 8) and work Rounds 1–4 of the pattern. Work in the colour sequence shown here. Make a total of 52 flowers.

Slip stitch the flowers together along the chain loops. Connect all the chain loops, only leaving the edge loops unworked.

Weave in all the ends and carefully steam the scarf into shape.

Wrist warmers

warming. wonderful. woolly.

Size: 25cm (9¾in) long (with edging); 8.5cm (3⅓in) wide • Level of difficulty **

Materials

- Wool/cashmere blend (55% merino ultra-fine, 33% acrylic, 12% cashmere, length 125m/50g, 136¾yd/1¾oz): 100g (3½oz) in your chosen colour (e.g. cream, natural, beige or blue-grey)
- Crochet hook no. 4/E US (3.5mm)
- Sewing thread in a matching colour and a sewing needle

Gauge

1 crocheted square = approximately 7.5 x 7.5cm (3 x 3in)

How it's done

Work in your chosen colour. To make a square, create a magic ring using a double loop (see page 8) and work Rounds 1–4 of Pattern 1. Work a total of six squares, and sew each set of three squares together to make two strips.

Now work 1 row of 1 double crochet (UK treble), 2 chain in turn down the long sides. Sew the strips together along the long sides. Work trim along the top edge of the wrist warmers as shown in Pattern 2.

Crochet pattern 1

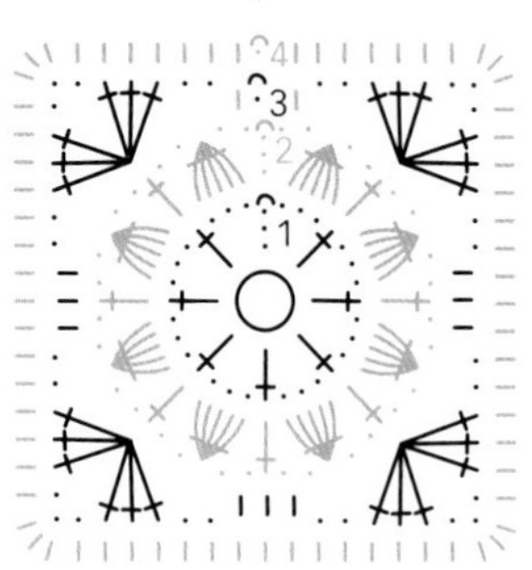

Crochet pattern 2

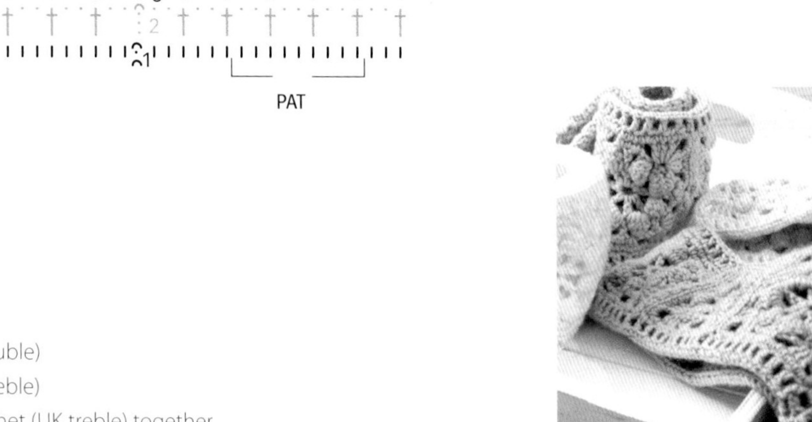

Symbols

- · = 1 chain
- ⌒ = 1 slip stitch
- I = 1 single crochet (UK double)
- † = 1 double crochet (UK treble)
- = decrease 3 double crochet (UK treble) together
- o = 1 picot (3 chain, 1 slip stitch into first chain)

PAT = Pattern repeat

Patchwork throw

plush. pastel. pretty.

Size: 115 x 165cm (45¼ x 65in) • Level of difficulty **

Materials

- Wool blend with cashmere (55% wool, 33% polyacrylic, 12% cashmere, length 25m/50g, 27½yd/1¾oz): 1000g (35¼oz) blue-grey (main colour of crochet squares and back), approximately 100g (3½oz) each in grey, lilac, brown, light grey, pale pink, dark grey, slate, yellow, beige, light blue, soft pink, soft lilac (colours for the middles of the crochet squares)
- Crochet hook no. 6 US (4mm)

Gauge

1 crocheted square = 16 x 16cm (6¼ x 6¼in)

Colour sequence of square

Round 1–7: One colour for the middle

Round 8–9: Blue-grey

Symbols

- · = 1 chain
- ⌒ = 1 slip stitch
- ı = 1 single crochet (UK double)
- T = 1 half double crochet (UK half treble)
- † = 1 double crochet (UK treble)
- ⌡ = 1 relief double crochet (UK relief treble) from front
- ǂ = 1 treble crochet (UK double treble)

If the symbols are joined at the bottom, this means the stitches are worked into the same stitch of the previous round.

How it's done

To make a square, create a magic ring using a double loop (see page 8) and work Rounds 1–9 of Pattern 1 in the sequence of colours indicated, and always working only into the back loop of the stitch in Round 8. The pattern is only complete to Round 4; add Rounds 5–9 as shown in the sketched half.

Work a total of 77 squares. Slip stitch the squares together in blue-grey in eleven rows of seven squares. Now crochet 6 rows of relief double crochet (UK relief trebles) around the front of the throw, working 2 relief double crochet (UK relief trebles), 2 chain, 2 relief double crochet (UK relief trebles) into the corner stitch. Then work a border in blue-grey to Pattern 2 into the relief double crochet (UK relief trebles).

Weave in all the ends and steam the throw to shape it.

Crochet pattern 1

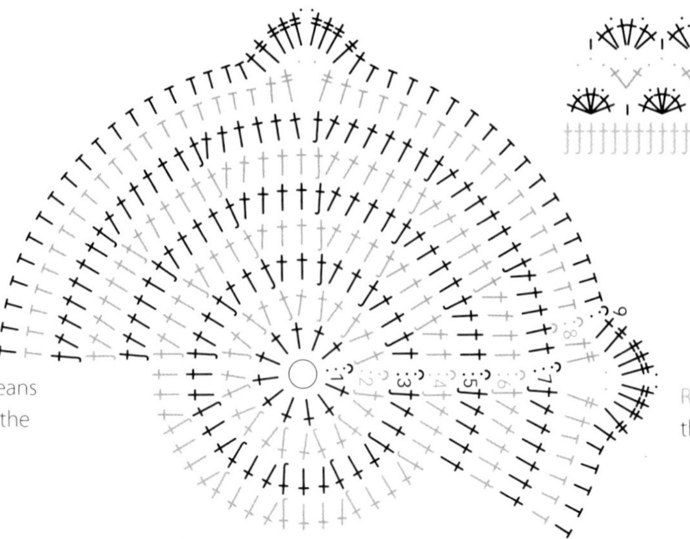

Crochet pattern 2

MS

Round 8: Always work into the back loop of the stitch.